1894/95 - 2000/2001

LLANDRINDOD WELLS URBAN DISTRICT COUNCIL
LLANDRINDOD WELLS TOWN COUNCIL

THE COUNCIL WISHES JOEL WILLIAMS
EVERY SUCCESS WITH THIS BOOK

Photograph - the late Mr. Arthur Pembridge

LLANDRINDOD WELLS SIGNAL BOX MUSEUM
OPEN FROM SPRING BANK HOLIDAY
UNTIL AUGUST BANK HOLIDAY
FRIDAYS AND SATURDAYS
11.00 AM TO 12.30 PM AND 1.30 PM TO 3.00 PM

FOREWORD

In compiling this volume of "Voices Of Llandrindod Wells", I have taken a range of themes concerning everyday life in the last century in Llandrindod Wells. They are:
Childhood, Education, Health, Work, Trade, Transport, Leisure and Entertainment. I realise there are many more themes yet to explore but I hope the reader will enjoy the glimpses of peoples' lives as they grew up, lived and worked in Llandrindod Wells. As far as I know, the facts as related to me are correct but where written data was not available, exact corroboration of dates is difficult.

Joel Williams

ACKNOWLEDGEMENTS

Red Dragon Press, H.A.N.D Graphics, Radnorshire Museum, Powys Archives, Castle Media, Llandrindod Wells Town Council, Llandrindod Wells Town Trust, National Cycle Museum, Mr. Don Nelson, Mrs. Ruth Jones, Mr. & Mrs. Bumford, Mr. Tom Norton, Mrs. Kathleen Davies, Elaine Matheson, The Late Miss Mary E. Abberley, The Late Mr. Jack Saunders, The Late Mr. & Mrs. Duff Edwards, Marina Thornett - Red Dragon Press. Also may I thank all of the advertisers and the many other people who have helped me with the publication of this book.

To set the following scenes, here is a travel writer's first impression of Llandrindod Wells taken from "In Search Of Wales" by H.V. Morton 1932.

"It is a Spa set in a garden. Nature has shot up its medicinal waters in a rustic glen, and the municipality has, with more than municipal wisdom, improved and cultivated the surroundings.
I went to the pump-room in the park and tried a glass of Saline, which I thought pleasant and - just the sort of thing a doctor would offer when there is nothing seriously wrong with you."

"I was interested in the Spa's most recent measure, one of the latest and most expensive X-ray outfits in the country. You stand behind a kind of screen, there is a flare of light and those on the other side of the screen can see through your head or any other part of you."

Chalybeate Well at Rock Park - 1906

Another amusing and interesting account was given to me by Mrs. E. Crompton who until recently lived at lakeside.

It was recalled by her brother-in-law, a Mr. Byron Morris of South Wales and gives us an insight into the thrills of a holiday in the town as seen through the eyes of a small boy.

Charabanc - Elan Valley Photograph Company
From Mrs E. Crompton

A WEEK IN HEAVEN

"One week a year, benevolent employers would give their workers a week off (unpaid in most cases) which was called Stop Week and which usually fell on the first week in August. Those people who could afford it, after saving up their meagre wages for a whole year, would leave the smoke and grime of the valleys and make for the fresh air of the country. This need was provided by towns like Llandeilo, Aberystwyth and Llandrindod. Llandrindod obviously saw the potential of this lucrative trade and spent a lot of capital in building some very fine hotels, in and around the town."

"My first glimpse of this heavenly place came at the age of eleven years when my aunt, uncle and cousin Marion packed our two large suitcases, one with clothes, and the other with food. We made our way down to Victoria station in Swansea (where the Leisure Centre is situated now) on the tram and boarded the train to Llandrindod Wells. The journey was endless, stopping at such places as Llandeilo, Builth Road and under the tunnel below the Sugarloaf mountain and it seemed that we would never get to our destination. We were told that the town band would be meeting us but I cannot recollect this happening at all."

"My first impression of this wonderland was the cleanliness and freshness of everything and the wonderful clean hotels. I had never seen such beautiful buildings before in my life! We made our way to Ridgebourne where we were to stay with Mrs. Tim Williams who had a three storey house with a bay window. It was situated on the right hand side of the road leading to the lake. On the opposite side of the road was a large emporium called "Edwards" shop and just below was a greengrocery where the ladies acquired their vegetables for the forthcoming feasting."

"Mrs. Williams was a very nice person and she made us all tea and cakes. Her husband, Tim, was part-time Town Crier and would dress up in his uniform and ring his bell every night at six o clock when he would shout the news of the day to the town, forecast the weather and announce forthcoming attractions."

"Having unpacked our bags, it was time to explore the wonders of the town. As it was Saturday afternoon the town was heaving with people shopping for the Sunday food, which the landladies would cook for their guests, I think they also charged ten shillings a week for the room!!"

"I went off to explore the wonders of the Rock Park by a lane leading from Ridgebourne via some fields. I discovered some birds' nests with beautiful coloured eggs in them but I carefully replaced them in their nests. When I arrived near the park there was an orchestra playing in the pavilion and I sat on the grass enjoying the music. They were playing some Gilbert and Sullivan excerpts, which I thoroughly enjoyed. I then went down to the spring, which ran from a spout in the wall with an iron mug secured with a chain. This particular well dispensed Chalybeate water. I made a cup out of my hands (not wanting to drink from the iron mug) and drank. It tasted funny but not unpleasant. It was said that at one time, they tried to sell this water, but the well ran dry so they stopped, and ever since the water has been free and has not stopped running. It must have done me some good because I have reached the age of eighty eight and am still going strong."

"My next venture was up to the lake. On the way I found some bushes with raspberries on. Whether they were wild or once cultivated in an old garden I don't know but they tasted very nice and I had a handful. When I arrived at the lake there were lots of people sailing in punts and beautifully varnished boats and it was great fun watching some of the sailors trying to row, some going around in circles and others clinging desperately to their punt poles. There was an occasional splash as someone fell into the water. Great fun!"

"On Tuesday we were up bright and early as we were going in Tom Norton's "Charabanc" (picture enclosed) to see the wonders of the Elan Valley's Birmingham water works. Sandwiches were prepared and packed, thermos flasks of tea were packed in carrier bags. We arrived at

Tom Norton's garage and the charabanc was waiting. The driver then swung the handle in front of the vehicle and took his rightful place at the steering wheel and with a full compliment we were off."

"The roads were not very good, with pot holes that had to be avoided, even as far as driving on to the other side of the road but there was very little traffic and when the odd car went past, the drivers would wave to each other in a friendly greeting."

"We proceeded through the town of Rhayader and on to the Elan Valley. We were not disappointed with the wonderful sight that met us. The large stretches of water were something I had never seen before. The top dam was especially dramatic and we were able to walk across it to the other side."

"We had our picnic lunch and spent a few hours at this delightful spot and then it was time to go back to Llandrindod. We stopped outside a pub in Rhayader for the men to have a pint but the ladies stayed outside because they did not go into pubs in those days. However, glasses of lemonade were brought out for the ladies and I had one too."

"On our way back we had a shower of rain so the driver stopped the bus, and assisted by some of the men in the party, succeeded in raising the enormous canopy over our heads which kept the people sitting in the middle of the bus dry. Those on the outside became a bit damp. A singsong was started on the way back with songs such as "One man went to mow" "Old McDonald had a farm" etc. We eventually arrived back at our lodgings, where Mrs. Williams had prepared supper for us and a good time was had by all."

"On the Wednesday we all went for a long walk to "Shaky Bridge". Not very exciting for me, but they all seemed to enjoy it. In the evening we went to a cinema in Middleton Street called the "Kino". After queuing for what seemed like a long time to me, we eventually took our seats. I have forgotten the name of the film but I remember the boiled sweets that my aunt gave us to suck."

Shaky Bridge

"On Thursday I decided to take a walk up to the golf course and watch the antics of some of the beginners. It was most amusing, this course was more in keeping with mountaineering than golfing but there were wonderful views overlooking the surrounding countryside. The lazy golfers were brought up to the club by a Ford van converted to carry people and called "Colonel Bogey". In the afternoon we all went down to watch the Bowls tournament. There were lots of games in progress and some very keen players. I understand that the games are still a popular feature of the town."

"On Friday I went for a walk to Middleton Street to look at the shops with funny postcards on racks. It did not cost anything to look at them and have a good laugh. I walked around to the Metropole Hotel, where on the croquet lawn across the road, men in white clothes were playing the game in all seriousness."

"In the evening there was a Carnival atmosphere with hundreds of people dancing in the street to jazz bands. As this was our last night of the holiday, everyone was out to enjoy themselves - including me - I had never seen anything like it before and the memory of that night has always remained with me."

"Saturday morning was the time to pack our bags and make for the station and back to those "dark satanic mills." Sadly we said goodbye to Llandrindod as the train made it's way back to Swansea."

"In later years when we had a car, one of the first trips we took was to Llandrindod and were saddened to see those wonderful Hotels, turned into offices and all sorts of other uses. The beautiful lake covered with weeds held no sign of a boat, the shop fronts were boarded up and an air of desolation hung over the whole town. I hope that some day it will resume it's former glory."

Byron Morris.

Temple Gardens & Metropole Hotel

What Better Place To Start Than On My Own Doorstep!

The Crossing

"The area of Llandrindod known as the crossing, consists of the North Ward of the town and is so called because of the railway level crossing. A signal box and a small cottage used to stand either side of the line, the cottage has long gone and the signal box was removed some years ago and rebuilt at Llandrindod station, where it can be visited by railway enthusiasts."

"Several businesses still trade at the crossing including a family grocery and post office established in 1904. It is served by a fish and chip shop, a garden machinery repair business, and a public house."

"Long gone is the brickyard at the bottom of Brookland Road - now a housing estate, and gone also is the Baptist Chapel in Waterloo Road. The Dinam football field is now the site of various factories including Maxwell Engineering and the cornfields where the corncrake was common are now the Waterloo Road Industrial estate. Even the fields I played in twenty years ago have disappeared under new housing and the lapwings that nested there are long gone."

J. HODGES
TREMONT ROAD,
LLANDRINDOD WELLS
TEL: 01597 82 2239
ESTABLISHED 1904

INCLUDING:
TREMONT POST OFFICE
"NEW BIGGER OFFICE"

GROCERS, OFF LICENCE
NEWSPAPERS,
MAGAZINES,
NATIONAL LOTTERY
AND INSTANTS

Mr. Don Nelson was brought up in the crossing area and told me many a good tale - the following are just a few.

"When we lived in Nelson Street the whole area was teeming with frogs. The sound of their croaking in the Spring was really loud. We locals got used to it but some of the visitors said it kept them awake at night. The story is that Mr. Percy Bufton and his cousin got some African frogs and let them loose in the brickyard pool, where - who knows, they bred because these frogs were big yellow ones and you could hear them all along Waterloo Road from the football field to the Dinam. Another wonderful sound down there was the call of the Corncrakes in the hayfields where the Mid Wales yarns factory is now."

Drawing By P.S.F Williams

"When we were kids we were told by our father to be in by nine o clock. In the summer he'd come outside and blow his trumpet - which I guess he learnt to play when he was in the forces during the First World War. We had to be home within half an hour - or else!
You could hear the trumpet for miles around! He was a big fellow and taught physical training in the rooms under the old Baptist Chapel in Waterloo Road. The Boy Scouts used to meet there and my mother was the last person to be baptized there."

"One of our favourite places to play was the brickyard pool at the bottom of Brookland Road. We'd build rafts and paddle them across the pool which was about 10-15 feet deep. In Winter, if the ice was thick enough, we'd skate."

"I remember one day, I suppose it was 1939, we were down by Cwmbach and the Sketty Oil Refinery in Swansea had been bombed overnight, - the smell of oil burning was quite strong as it was carried up here on the wind."

"Most of the local businesses had errand boys who rode push bikes with big front carriers and they wore white aprons. As a youngster I used to help Mr. Bert Sim's at the crossing and his old mother - not unlike Queen Victoria, used to send me on this bike down to the gas works in Ddole Road to fetch her a bag of coke. She gave me 1 shilling 11and a half d for the coke and told me to keep the change!, I think I was done there!"

"I remember the old Roman boat they found in the river. We kids used to swim off it - never knew what it was. It seemed like an old chunk of wood jammed tight by the bank at Inskip's Ford. Now it's in the museum of course."

"I had a few scrapes as a boy - ran into the lamp post in the middle of Fiveways after free-wheeling down Spa Road, but the worst was probably when I was sledging down the slope from the blacksmith past the Middleton Arms. A lorry was parked across the road and we'd been told by the headmaster of the school, not to do it but I had this go and as it was so icy I couldn't stop - went straight under the lorry, crossed the main road, hit the kerb and caterpulted myself through the hedge onto the railway embankment! - Oh, I was pulling blackthorn spikes out of myself for days after that!"

"When I was in the National School, Miss Mary Abberley was one of the teachers. I was sent up to Trefonnen Farm where she lived, to fetch the morning milk for school. Coming back down I slipped on some ice and spilt a lot of milk.

The blacksmith saw me crying and took me in to top it up with water! Well, Miss Abberley knew the milk wasn't right. She asked me if I'd spilt any and I told a fib and said "no." "Well what is all that frozen milk doing on the road?" she replied. I nearly died with shame!"

Mr. Don Nelson

Mr. Charles Jones - Blacksmith at Trefonnen Lane -
Courtesy of Radnorshire Museum

Also included in this Lot is

LLANFAWR FARMHOUSE,

containing Six Bed Rooms, Three Sitting Rooms, Kitchen and Offices ; Homestead with Cow Stalls, Barn, Three-stall Stable, Hovel and Piggeries. Also

TREFONEN FARMHOUSE,

stone and slated, and containing Seven Bed Rooms, Parlour, Kitchen, Dairy, &c. Farmery with Cowhouse, Barn, Stable and Hovel. Also

NEUADD FARM,

a stone and slated FARMHOUSE with Four Bed Rooms, Three Sitting Rooms ; Dairy, Barn, Stables, Cart Hovel and Cow Stalls.

The whole forming

A Very Valuable Building Estate.

And estimated to contain by Ordnance Survey

104 a.   3 r.   20 p.

It is believed that a Valuable Bed of Stone underlies this Lot.

Trefonnen Farm & Surrounding Area

Trefonnen Dairy Farm was one of the oldest buildings in the Llandrindod area, and was sadly demolished about twenty years ago after falling into much disrepair.
It was the childhood home of my contributor - the late Miss Mary E. Abberley.
The old National School site is occupied by Theatr Powys with the new Trefonnen primary school behind on a larger site.

Trefonnen Dairy Farm - 1900's

Theatr Powys - Copyright Joel Williams

The Pierrots

"My mother used to take visitors at Trefonnen Farm, where we lived, and every year the same two families came. They went down to the Rock Park once or twice to watch the Pierrots perform. The star of the show in my estimation, was the ventriloquist Arthur Prince with his wonderful doll. The Pierrots came every summer, staying in local apartments. They dressed up in their costumes and had big pointed hats with a tassel on the top."

"There were also orchestras coming to play, and one year it was an Irish ladies orchestra of about ten to twelve musicians wearing pale blue dresses and Irish green sashes. The pianist was an Italian lady called Madame Furio and we had three of them staying at Trefonnen Farm for the season. They would play afternoons and evenings then come back for a terrific supper, whilst we were in bed. My mother had a lot of clearing up to do in the morning!"

"The day war broke out Madame Furio decided to return home quickly!"

Miss M. Abberley

The Pierrots - Courtesy of S Collard

Pierrots At Rock Park - Courtesy Of Radnorshire Museum

David Lloyd George

"I remember going to a meeting with my father, he was very poorly then, and a cousin of mine said that he could die a happy man now that he'd shaken the hand of Lloyd George."

"My father was a dedicated Liberal, and worked hard for the Liberal cause in this area. The night before the election of 1910, I think it was, the Conservatives had a large meeting at the Pavilion and the Liberals had theirs in the Albert Hall."

"I remember we had staying with us a Mr. & Mrs. Harvey and their twenty year old daughter. They were Liberal supporters and after the election they sent my father a telegram saying, "Congratulations, you have won a great victory - Tory no good." I still have it today although it's pretty yellow with age. David Lloyd George used to stay at the Gwalia Hotel - a very popular hotel in those days!"

Miss Mary Abberley

Mr. David Lloyd George at a meeting - Courtesy of Radnorshire Museum

EDUCATION

The old County Primary School was in Oxford Road, off High Street and a few years ago was resited in new buildings in Cefnllys Lane.

Our present day High School is in Dyffryn Road and was preceded by the Grammar School in Alexandra Road. The College of Further Education was previously the Ye Wells Hotel and still bears most of the resemblance to the old hotel.

College Of Further Education
Previously The Ye Wells Hotel

School

"I went to the National School after it was built in 1913. We had a very strict headmaster but there were Christmas treats and outings to see anything interesting that was going on in the town. Playtimes and after school we'd play hopscotch and skipping, if we could get some boys to swing the big rope, - marbles were popular too. Our mothers would make little bags for us, to keep the lovely coloured marbles in."

"We had a sports day each year on Rock Ddole and I was quite good at jumping and running. The boys used to cheat in the sack race by pushing a hole in the sack - very comical!"

"At Trefonnen Farm we had a lovely field between us and the quarry called Green field, now the housing estate. It had a small croquet lawn and the Baptist Sunday School teas were held there. My mother boiled the kettles for tea in the house and we'd take the hot tea up to tables at the top of the field"

Miss M. Abberley

National School 1938 - Courtesy of Ruth Jones

PROGRAMME, ONE PENNY.

Llandrindod Wells Elementary Schools.

FIRST ANNUAL

ATHLETIC SPORTS

ON THE ROCK PARK HOTEL GROUNDS,

On Wednesday, July 29th, 1914, at 2-15 p.m.

President—J. LUTHER GREENWAY, ESQ.

MRS. RISING, Greenway Manor, will kindly distribute the Prizes

Judges: Rev. R. W. F. Singers-Davies, Councillor T. Evans,
Hon. Secs.: D. Morris, D. Jones.

ENTRANCE TO THE FIELD 6d. EACH. ALL ELEMENTARY SCHOOL CHILDREN FREE.

LIST OF EVENTS

BOYS' RACE, 50 YARDS HANDICAP, UNDER 8 YEARS.

1st HEAT.

Stanley Francis	....	Scratch.
Norman Milward	,,	,,
Reginald Hamer	,,	,,
Alen Breese	,,	2 yards.
Albert Knill	,,	2 yards.
Reggie Pritchard	,,	4 yards.

3rd Heat.

Thos. Rogers	....	Scratch.
Cecil Morris	,,	,,
James Martin	,,	2 yards.
Alan Lloyd	,,	2 yards.
Walter Rogers	,,	4 yards.
Babbo Gibson	,,	4 yards.

2nd HEAT.

Wilfred Abberley	....	Scratch.
Morgan Milward	,,	,,
Wilfred Mundey	,,	2 yards.
Ivor Harries	,,	2 yards.
Willie Mills	,,	,,
Thos. Jones	,,	4 yards.

4th HEAT.

Gordon Lloyd	....	Scratch.
Miah Abberley	,,	,,
Alick Bonnd	,,	,,
Miah Hope	,,	,,
David Blake	,,	,,
Donald Jones	,,	3 yards.

BOYS' RACE, 120 YARDS, HANDICAP...OPEN TO SCHOLARS OF BOTH SCHOOLS.

THE WINNER OF THE 100 YARDS HANDICAP AND THE WINNER OF THE 100 YARDS SCRATCH RACE WILL EACH BE PUT BACK 3 YARDS IN THIS RACE.

1st HEAT.

Stanley Wilde	....	Scratch.
Tom Powell	,,	,,
John Gittoes	,,	3 yards.
Walter Vaughan	,,	,,
William Rogers	,,	,,
John Knill	,,	,,
Ernest Lewis	,,	9 yards.
Edward Powell	,,	,,

4th HEAT.

Fred Roberts	....	Scratch.
Harold Humphreys	,,	,,
John Bound	,,	3 yards.
Willie Abberley	,,	,,
George Thomas	,,	,,
Eric Binyon	,,	8 yards.
Arthur Selwyn	,,	,,
Harry Partridge	,,	,,

2nd HEAT.

Jack Pritchard	....	3 yards.
Harold Jones	,,	,,
Dilwyn Watkins	,,	6 yards.
Cecil Breeze	,,	,,
Jim Mason	,,	9 yards.
Jack Maldwin	,,	,,
Wm. Davies	,,	,,
Griff. Watkin	,,	,,

5th HEAT.

Eric Jones	....	6 yards.
Fred Thomas	,,	,,
Lionel Beard	,,	9 yards.
Reggie Knill	,,	,,
E. Lewis	,,	,,
Maldvyn Roberts	,,	,,
Stanley Gough	,,	,,
Jim Watkins	,,	12 yards.

3rd HEAT.

Archie Norton	....	Scratch.
Edward Shipley	,,	3 yards.
Douglas Jones	,,	6 yards.
Austin Sheen	,,	,,
Lawrence Jones	,,	,,
Leslie Brick	,,	9 yards.
Douglas Humphreys	,,	,,
Arthur McBride	,,	,,

6th HEAT.

Leslie Small	....	Scratch.
Edwin Rogers	,,	,,
George Evans	,,	6 yards.
Claud Gough	,,	,,
Walter Rogers	,,	9 yards.
Seth Botwood	,,	,,
Wilfred Powell	,,	,,

GIRLS' THREE-LEGGED RACE—FINAL.

1st .... 2nd .... 3rd ....

BOYS' 120 YARDS HANDICAP—FINAL.

1st .... 2nd .... 3rd ....

HIGH JUMP GIRLS.

Marjorie Lewis.	Lena Wilde.
Gertrude Breese.	Ada Breese.
Cissy Lewis.	Sybil Atherton.
Edith Bate.	Alice Ashley.
Florence Mason.	Violet Carr.
Ida Morris.	Olwen Jones.
Ethel Botwood.	May Jones.
Lulu Breese.	Dorothy Wilkins.
Hetty Malcolm.	Joan Oliver.
Mary Abberley.	Gwen Williams.

Athletic Sports Day Programme 1914 - Courtesy Of Ruth Jones

The National School 1940 - Courtesy Of Ruth Jones

The National School 1940

The following list of names are some of the people in the photograph, supplied by Mr. Derek Gough

Mr. Harvey Jones, Derek Jones, Tom Evans, David Heighway, Tom Powell, David Llewelyn, Donald Janrell, Billy Heighway, Glyn Watson, Donald Hodges, Eric Nelson & Donald Davies

Ruth Jones, B Vaughan, Nora Reynolds, Barbara Morris, Beryl Gough & Mary Jones

Also in the photograph are the students from Cheltenham Ladies College.

Education

The Llandrindod and Cefnllys National School (now Trefonnen School) was opened in 1878. The Master was a Mr. Quarterman and I have a list of the terms that were charged. It was 6d for one child, 9d for two children, 11d for three and an extra 2d for every additional child in a family.

"I went to the school, of course, and later taught there for many years. It had one very long room with three classes in and an adjacent room divided into two for the infants."

"In my time Mr. Cooper was headmaster and very strict he was too! Three of the Maine family from Dan-Y-Graig Farm taught there as well, two sisters and a brother. The brother was a Mr. Tom Maine and he went on to London and became a teacher at the Royal College of Music!"

Miss M. Abberley

"After I retired from Trefonnen School - quite by chance, I was asked to be an invigilator for exams at the College of Further Education. I also used to invigilate the police officers' promotion exams, but had to retire from that when I turned 70."

Miss M. Abberley

Headmaster - Mr. Donald Davies with school children and the Late Miss Abberley.

Miss Mary E. Abberley was presented with this clock in recognition of her services to Llandrindod Wells National School from 1920 - 1963 on her retirement as Deputy Headteacher on July 19th 1963.

Education & Sport

"I used to go to the old school in Oxford Road. There were several private schools in town at that time and my sister went to one in Broadway. There was another at the Lindens I think and we used to call them the Red Caps on account of the berets they wore."

"I went to the County Secondary School. I was very keen on sport, lots of cross country and I won the "Victor Ludorum" several years. I used to run the mile and 100 yards, high jump and when the lake was frozen in the winter I played ice hockey. Mr. Tom Norton senior was a keen skater - used to see him up there. It was sixpence to go skating and Mr. Bertford the boatman in charge during the summer, collected the money."

Mr. Duff Edwards

"We all went to Sunday School, of course, at Holy Trinity, where my Grandfather was a church warden and there would be annual Sunday School outings. The most enjoyable trip was with the Bible class to Stratford-Upon-Avon. Major Mostyn who was Director of Education for the County took that class."

"We used to go caddying on the Golf Links - charging the golfers 1s 9d to carry their bags round, and later it went up to 1s 11d. Sometimes you'd hang around for hours waiting to be selected so I always took a bottle of cold tea and a hot cross bun with me. If a visiting golfer thought well of you - you could be hired for the week and always got a good tip at the end of it."

"There was also a lot of Clay Pigeon shooting up by the Golf Links. It must have been UK Championships I think but the "pop-pop-pop" would go on all week. In the town there would be bowling tournaments and at that time, nearly all the houses in Llandrindod seemed to be boarding houses. Such was the number of visitors coming there was a newspaper printed just to let everyone know which families, and where they were staying - very grand!"

"Ye Wells Hotel used to have one or two lifts complete with lift girls dressed in uniforms"

Mr. Don Nelson

Childhood & Work

"We lived at Three Wells, Howey and supplied Llandrindod with milk and eggs, and also some meat. My father was a slaughter man as well, and bred and killed his own animals. We'd take the meat round with the milk to sell it. Milk was five pence in old money for a pint and when I was too young to drive a vehicle, I had a little horse and float with a big chair in the front. The milk was poured out of a brass tap which had to be kept shining and clean. You were never allowed to go to the front door of a house - it was always the tradesmen's entrance round the back. The milk wasn't in bottles you had to go in and get a jug to measure a pint out. Some people only gave me jam jars to put it in. To keep the milk cool at home, we'd keep the churn in the brook. This is why we had to come into town twice a day - there were no fridges in those days. If it was thundery weather the milk wouldn't keep until the next day."

"We reared chickens and geese too and a dozen eggs were nine pence - of course some people wanted thirteen to the dozen!
My mother had thirty geese to sell one Christmas, she was offered ten shillings each for them and refused because they were really good ones, so she ended up taking them all the way to Builth but still she could get no more than ten shillings so she brought them back again and sold them to a shop.
You see, there was a lot of work involved in geese. There was an old house at Three Wells where the feathering was done. It had an old fashioned black grate which was lit on feathering day and neighbours would come round to help. Great excitement it was, and we used to run home from school to join in, as we didn't usually see so many people."

Kathleen Davies

Drawing By Mrs. J. Williams

HEALTH

The provision of healthcare in Llandrindod is supplied by the Llandrindod Wells Hospital, now a much enlarged building, and a doctors' surgery in Spa Road East. The introduction of the National Health Service after the Second World War must have been one of the greatest changes to peoples lives during the last century.

Hospitals & Doctor Bowen

"I recall, when the hospital was first built, after the First World War. I think they used to give you a ticket, which cost a guinea and if you needed to be admitted you paid another 7s 6d. There were quite a few doctors in town - one was Doctor Bowen whose residence is now the Town Hall. He had his own dispensary and made up his own medicines as they did in those days.
I remember the Scarlet Fever outbreak when I was teaching. The isolation hospital was down by the cemetery, where the allotments are now."

Miss M. Abberley

"In my mother's day there was a Diptheria epidemic here and she lost two sisters and a brother at the time. They're buried up in the old graveyard.
I remember Highland Moors being used as a convalescent hospital during the Great War."

Mr. Duff Edwards

Mr. Jack Saunders recalls what one could expect from a visit to the dentist in the 1920's.

"I went to a dentist in Park Crescent, next to Lockes the greengrocers. He never gave sedatives - he just pulled them out"

Mr. J. Saunders

Hospital - Courtesy of Radnorshire Museum

Copyright Joel Williams

Town Hall Illuminated For The Coronation Of George VI in 1937
- Courtesy of Radnorshire Museum

Copyright - Joel Williams

WORK & TRADE

In the early half of the last century, the largest employers were probably the hotels and associated service industries. Nowadays of course these account for less jobs, with the emphasis on modern industries and local government providing the largest opportunities for employment.

Post Offices

"The first Post Office my mother would have remembered was on High Street where Powerprint Printers is now. Then it was moved to the corner of Park Terrace. To my mother, the High Street was the main street - I don't suppose there was much at all in Middleton Street in those days.".

Miss M. Abberley

Llandrindod Post Office In Park Crescent

Working At The Post Office

"When I was a Post Office messenger boy we covered a vast area from Radnor Forest, Abbeycwmhir, Builth Road and over the Golf Links to Gilwern."

"Later on after the war, during the 1947 snow storms, I'd drive the van up to Rhayader, Pantydwr and St. Harmon then back to Rhayader and up the Elan Valley. There were a lot of Irishmen there, building the new dam and they'd ask me to give them a lift into town. They added weight to the back of the van - which made driving in those conditions much easier and they were handy with their shovels too."

"The only fat things up there that year were dogs and buzzards - there were dead sheep everywhere.
The other lads would say I was lucky as they were snowed up to their elbows that week. The only way to get across the drifts was to put my cape down and roll, if you tried to walk you'd sink in. Some of the by-lanes still had a bit of snow in them until June!"

Mr. Don Nelson

Middleton Street 1947 - Courtesy of Radnorshire Museum

Post Office Workers 1930's - Courtesy Of Mr. Don Nelson

"When I started work for the Post Office in the 1930's I was a telegram boy. We worked like little bluebottles, delivering the telegrams on our bicycles. The Post Office in those days was opposite the Gwalia buildings on the corner of Park Crescent - the property is now flats."

"The new Post Office was built, and soon after we all had our photograph taken in the yard. I suppose about thirty people worked there then. When I started work I got six shillings a week going up to nine shillings after twelve months. - I thought I was a millionaire! Some days I would take out up to twenty telegrams especially if there was a local wedding on. I used to bring all the mail from the station to the old Post Office on a hand truck off the morning train and take the local mail to the train again in the evening. It was hard work until we got vans."

Mr. D. Nelson

Post Office Working

"When war broke out I was working at the hospital but left soon after. There was plenty of jobs in those days, they couldn't get enough staff. The chap at the post office said I was just the man they were looking for so I started the next morning. I'd be meeting the five o' clock mail train and then later I'd put the mail for away on a midday train. The last of the mail would go on the nine o' clock evening train and about nine thirty I'd put the van away."

"They were teaching a lot of women to drive because of the shortage of men, due to the war. They had to learn where all the letter boxes were and the different collection times as we were tied to time you know. We weren't supposed to go faster than 30mph but if you got held up somewhere you had to get a move on! You had to be back to get mail on the train."

"It was good wages though, I had four times as much in my first week than I'd had the week before due to double time after so many hours.
We worked bank holidays too, even on Christmas day there was a delivery. It was double time for all bank holidays or you could take days in lieu. I always took the third week in January if nobody senior wanted that week, it always seemed to snow."

Mr. Jack Saunders

The Quarry

View Of The Quarry - Courtesy Of Radnorshire Museum

"There used to be a bridge across the main Tremont Road and the trucks came down from the quarry on rollers and ropes, one truck bringing the stone and another going back up. The stone was taken away by rail in those days."

"There were no houses between the road and the quarry then - just a big bank. The trucks' speed was regulated by a lever at the top, so that they didn't come down too fast. The quarry belonged to a Mr. Thomas Lant, who also owned another one at Builth Wells."

"He supplied stone for the roads as there was no tarmac then - just rough stone rolled in. He was a very kind man, and gave lots of people including me, allotments up Lant Avenue before any houses were built there. They went all the way to the quarry.
He also owned the Gorse Farm - it was mostly bog, soaking wet, but he drained the land and you could always be sure of a bag of peat from

there. It's the same brook that joins the one from the quarry and flows through the Town Hall gardens."

"When I came here to live in 1920, the visitors were coming back in great numbers after the Great War. In August, if they didn't book, they had nowhere to go and I used to see them sitting on the windowsills of the Hampton looking lost."

Mr. Jack Saunders

Quarry Bridge

"The quarry bridge used to be where the telephone exchange is now. The stones from the quarry used to come down in trucks and would then be tipped into bigger trucks on the railway side of the road. I lived at Trefonnen Farm, near the quarry and someone always came to warn us when they were going to blast so we could stay indoors until it was finished."

Miss M. Abberley

"Where it has now been levelled off we can remember the huge crushers there with a fifty foot drop. John can also remember a huge fire up there which he watched from the windows of Stoneleigh where he was living at the time. We both remember the bridge going over the road from the bottom of quarry lane (where the telephone exchange is now).
Trucks used to go over this taking sand and chippings from the quarry to be weighed on the weigh-bridge near the Countrywide stores."

Mr. & Mrs. Bumford

Quarry Bridge - Decorated For H.R.H. Edward Prince Of Wales 1926
Courtesy Of Radnorshire Museum

Copyright - Joel Williams

Station Yard

Looking back to the heydays of the railway when commodities such as coal came by rail, one can imagine the bustle of station yard with its coal merchants yards and offices and the loading and unloading of cattle. It was still used as an oil and petrol depot in my own memory, before the Kwik Save Supermarket was built on the site of the storage tanks. Eric Evans Car Sales took over and renovated the old good's shed building and now we also have the Countrywide Stores and the site of the Friday outdoor market.

"The Station Yard was a busy place at one time. There were gates at both ends which were locked at night. Quite a few coal merchants had depots there and where Eric Evans Car Sales is now was a big good's shed."

"There were stables for the dray horses - later it was all lorries, of course, as coal was brought in by road instead of the railway. Even petrol was brought in by rail at one time and where the market is on a Friday there were cattle pens for the loading and unloading of livestock."

Mr. Saunders

Copyright - Joel Williams

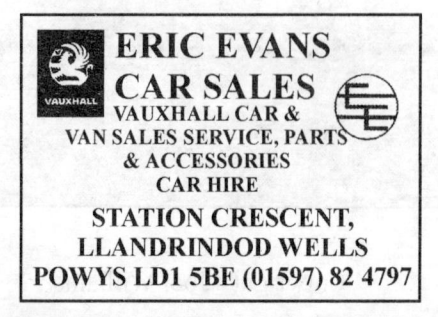

ERIC EVANS
CAR SALES
VAUXHALL CAR &
VAN SALES SERVICE, PARTS
& ACCESSORIES
CAR HIRE
STATION CRESCENT,
LLANDRINDOD WELLS
POWYS LD1 5BE (01597) 82 4797

Industry, Coal Yards & Council Horses

"There used to be quite a few coal hauliers in town - coal being the main fuel in those days. There were coal yards at the Crossing and quite a lot in Station Yard with horse drawn carts for deliveries. Mills and Breeze are just two of the companies that come to mind."

"The council also used a few horses, which they stabled at the back of Nelson Street and grazed them on the fields that are now the Housing Estate (The Project). There was a field by the Brickyard called the Grading Field. They used to graze cattle there until they were moved to Rhayader or Penybont markets.
The people taking in visitors for the summer didn't like the mess on the road. If we waited for them to come back in the evening, we might be given a ride on one of those huge horses - about 16-17 hands high I should think."

Mr. D. Nelson

"I moved with my parents to Wyvern Terrace in 1905 and remember, as a little girl, watching the council horses come home in the evenings. They'd be led up the rear lane to the stables, which are still there but used as garages now. Each horse would "spend a penny" in the yard before being taken in, they were very well trained weren't they!"

The Late Miss Annie Hutt of Wyvern Terrace, Waterloo Road

More Rain Must Come!
SPECIAL OFFER
35,000 RUBBER CAP COVERS,
KHAKI COLOR.

TO BE CLEARED AT 6½D EACH WORTH 2/-

IN 20 doz. LOTS 5/11 doz. COST DOUBLE.

AS ILLUSTRATION.

Good line for Cyclists, Motorists, Carters and Field Workers.

Terms :- Nett Spot Cash Ipswich.

AUGUSTUS POPE & CO.,
A. R. M. POPE SOLE PROPRIETOR,
WHOLESALE WAREHOUSEMEN,
IPSWICH.

Courtesy - Powys Archives

TO CARTERS.

WANTED

BY THE

LLANDRINDOD WELLS URBAN DISTRICT COUNCIL,

A LABOURER,

Capable of taking charge of Horse and Cart, and to act as Foreman Carter. Wages £1 3s. per week.

Applications, in own handwriting, stating age, experience, etc., to be delivered at the Offices of the Clerk to the Council, Town Hall, not later than November 13th, 1913.

C. C. Hughes, Printer, Middleton Street, Llandrindod Wells.

Courtesy - Powys Archives

TOWN HALL STABLES
LLANDRINDOD WELLS.

Messrs. BUFTON & SON

Are instructed to offer for Sale by Public Auction,

On Tuesday, 11th May, 1915,

At THREE o'clock p.m.

A VERY USEFUL BLACK

Cart GELDING

10 YEARS OLD.

Auctioneers' Office, Llandrindod Wells.

Printed at the " Standard " Office, Llandrindod Wells.

Courtesy - Powys Archives

Steam Laundry & Pump House Hotel

"There were several steam laundries in those days, each employing eight t ten people. Of course there was a big demand for them by all the hotels."

Miss M. Abberley

Steam Laundry At Dyffryn Road - Courtesy Of Radnorshire Museum

Pump House Hotel & Rock Park Hotel

The Pump House Hotel was probably the largest and finest of the Spa Hotels sited as it was beneath the wooded hillside with its own pump house for the Spa waters and a bandstand situated in the drive to the front. In later years it became the headquarters of Powys County Council but was demolished to make way for the present administrative complex. One of my contributors, the late Mr. Jack Saunders, recalls his first job as a gardener there in the 1920's. For the reader's interest, I am printing a touching account from Mrs. Ellen Phillips collected by Mrs. Ruth Jones, of the experiences of a young kitchen maid in the 1890's.

The Grand Pump House Hotel

Housemaid At Ye Wells
By Mrs. Ellen Phillips

"I was born near Leominster, and when I left school at the age of 14, I worked for a short while at the Royal Oak Hotel in that town. I had only been there a few weeks when another waitress told me all about Llandrindod and the Ye Wells Hotel. She had worked there the previous season and suggested that if I wrote to Mrs. Bryan Smith, the owner, I might get a job there. I did this and I soon received a letter from her saying that they could do with a housemaid on the first floor and offered me the job - she even sent me the 5/- rail fare!"

"When I arrived at Llandrindod station where was great activity all around. The "fly" from the Pump House Hotel was there to meet guests, and the van from the Ye Wells. The van took my tin box containing all my worldly belongings but I had to walk. I had never been further than Leominster in my life and I remember walking past the Metropole Hotel and imagining that Llandrindod must be like London. I rang the bell at Ye Wells and a page boy answered and took me to the reception desk. This was opposite the main door at the head of the stairs. The office on the right hand side of the stairs, where the book keeper worked. I was taken down to the staff room for tea, where everyone turned and looked me over. I was so shy that I told myself I would take the next train back home! (However, I stayed for over ten years.)"

"I arrived just before the season started and we had to light fires in every room to "air" all the mattresses and pillows - no central heating in those days! This took a whole fortnight and then all the rooms had a thorough cleaning to be ready for visitors. The season was from March - October.
We had to go on duty at 6.30 a.m. to do our calls. These were ordered the evening before - e.g a cup of tea at 7.30 a.m. etc. Even if there were not many calls there were sitting rooms to clean. Unless arrangements had been made for baths to be inclusive, they had to be paid for separately.
Breakfast was at 8 a.m., then back upstairs at 8.30 and until 12 o' clock it would be sweeping and dusting bedrooms, cleaning bathrooms and helping the chambermaids make the beds. If guests were leaving there might be three or four rooms to clear out and make ready for the next visitors. We had to go for our lunch one at a time. In the same way, our "off duty" in the afternoon was shared - if I was off from 2 to 4 then another maid would be off from 4 to 6, so that one of us would always be on call. We all had to be back on duty at

6.30 p.m. as we had to check all the rooms and turn the beds down and if the guests had had a wash during the afternoon there were slop buckets to be emptied. Usually we managed to finish by eight, when we had supper and then sometimes a quick walk around the lake. Then back at 9.30 when Madam would come down to the staff hall to read prayers. We would all have to kneel on the floor with our heads on a chair. Everybody was there, waiters, boots, billiard markers, etc. And she always knew if anyone was missing. Madam was quite strict. If there had been a bit of a staff upset she would get us all together and stress "Remember, this is MY house and I am the mistress of it" However, this didn't happen very often."

"I earned 2/6 a week. This was helped out by tips if you were lucky, and of course we lived in free. We had to provide our uniforms though - cotton print with plain aprons for the morning and black with fancy aprons for the afternoon. We also had to take our turn to do late duty - I did until 11 p.m. three times a week.
All the family worked in the hotel - Master Clement, Master Earnest, Miss Winnie and Miss Rachel. When Master Earnest married Miss Griffiths, the vicar's daughter from Newbridge, she also was roped in to work. Unfortunately Master Clement was killed in the 1914-18 War. When the news came through Madam was in bed for days. Later the family had a perpetual light placed in the chancel of Holy Trinity Church in his memory.
When Miss Rachel was married it was my privilege to dress the bride. She wore a beautiful figured satin gown with matching shoes and a long veil. In the lounge of the hotel the couple stood under a canopy of flowers shaped like a bell to receive the guests. The staff had their own party the night before."

"Many wealthy and well-known people stayed at Ye Wells. I remember one couple from Liverpool (he owned a factory). We called his wife the "Queen of Diamonds". When she came down to dinner she wore them everywhere - rings, necklace, brooches, earrings and in her hair. One of us always had to wait to help her undress, so we got a good look at them. Dame Clara Butt often stayed at the hotel and even had her own private staircase entrance. Other guests included an Indian Princess whose brother was a famous cricketer, Mr and Mrs. Wallis who owned a chain of shops in London (she played golf all day) and I remember also seeing Mr. Lloyd George in town, wearing his "Inverness" and raising his hat to the ladies."

"On summer evenings, there were crowds walking around the lake, all in evening dress. On the Whitsun and August bank holidays Middleton Street would be crowded with colliers and their families from South Wales. Every week there would be a play in the Pavilion. It cost 6d to sit in the gallery. I can remember seeing "Tea for Two" at the Pavilion Theatre. Sometimes there were dances held there, but we had to get permission to go. Also there were concert parties in the Rock Park and Sacred Concerts were held every Sunday in the hotel itself."

"At the end of the season we had to find winter jobs elsewhere. There was no dole money in those days, so we had to do something. One winter I went to work in a restaurant in Cardiff and another time I went to Burton Manor in Cheshire, which was the home of Mr. and Mrs. Gladstone - he was the son of the Prime Minister. During the whole time I was at Ye Wells I stayed in Llandrindod for only one winter. I remember that very well because it was so cold and there was skating on the lake."

"I met my husband on a "blind date". My girl friend asked me to make up a foursome with her boyfriend and his pal. We married the following year and lived for 60 years in Cefn Cottage in Cross Gates."

(Mrs. "Bob" Phillips has been a choir member and "pillar" of Llanbadarn Fawr Church for many years. She was once the Rector's dancing partner in "Swan Lake")

Ye Wells Hotel

"The Pump House Hotel was considered the best and it also had its own pump room to provide water for its visitors. It employed a good, efficient work force and had a laundry of its own. Another laundry was called Nelsons at the rear of Bryncoed in Waterloo Road."

Mr. Jack Saunders

The Pump House Hotel

Pump House Hotel Being Demolished
- copyright Joel Williams

"The Metropole was then called the Bridge Hotel and the water from the stream that now comes out in the park used to flow across the road. There was some kind of footbridge I believe, that was before the Automobile Palace, and before there was a road around the lake, only a footpath existed.
I remember water running across the road near Fiveways - when it flooded, vehicles got stuck and shops were flooded."

Mr. Jack Saunders

The Bridge Hotel - Now The Metropole

Copyright - Joel Williams

Ye Wells Hotel, Now Coleg Powys
Copyright Joel Williams

Horse & Cart Outside The Rock House Hotel
Courtesy Of Radnorshire Museum

The Rock House Hotel

The Rock House Hotel Before Demolition
Copyright Joel Williams

The Metropole
Llandrindod Wells, Powys LD1 5DY

A.A. *** W.T.B

Telephone (01597) 823700 Facsimile (01597) 824828
E.mail: info@metropole.co.uk   Internet: http://www.metropole.co.uk

Family Owned Hotel in the beautiful Heart of Wales
Indoor Leisure Complex
Conference and Dinner/Dance Function Rooms
Restaurant and Bar Snack Facilities with
delicious food using local Welsh produce
Large Selection of Fine Wines, Beers and Spirits

LAUNDERETTE
&
DRY CLEANING
TEMPLE STREET,
LLANDRINDOD WELLS
01597 82 2876

OPENING TIMES
8.00 AM TILL 8.00 PM
7 DAYS A WEEK

Emporium

Many different businesses occupy the large site that was once the Emporium. They include Russell, Baldwin & Bright Estate Agents, the Red Cross shop, Phillip Curnow - Financial Advisors, The Travel Centre, The Dilraj Indian Restaurant, the Classic Shoe Shop and Wallis Electrics. This is one of my favourite buildings in Llandrindod and was built in 1881 by Manchester architects Smith & Heathcote under the instructions of Mr. William Thomas, whose thriving business started in the village of Penybont - five miles away. It became famous throughout the country for its varied departments. It was the superstore of the last century!

The Emporium Warehouse,
LLANDRINDOD WELLS,
FOR
High-Class Tailoring
At MODERATE PRICE.

Talented Cutter and Experienced Staff on the Premises.
SUITS AT A FEW HOURS' NOTICE.
Immense assortment of Tweeds and Coatings in Stock.
Ladies' Tailor-made Costumes a Speciality.
MADE OF WELSH TWEEDS, etc.
LAWN TENNIS GOODS—Ready-Made and to order.
LADIES' & GENTS' MACKINTOSHES—At Special Prices.
LADIES' & GENTS' CYCLING CAPES, &c.

Proprietor—W. THOMAS.

FROM
Wᴹ THOMAS,

CENTRAL WALES EMPORIUM & WELSH WOOLLEN WAREHOUSE.

MILLINERY
DRESSMAKING
TAILORING
AND
GENERAL
DRAPERY,
&c.

EST 1799.

PER *Vd Post* DATE

Mr. Morris
Upper Hergert
Kington
Herefordshire

CARRIAGE PAID.

LLANDRINDOD WELLS.
BRANCHES, PENYBONT & DOLAU STORES

Emporium

"I remember the Emporium with its different departments, all like separate shops, from grocery to tailoring. In the tailoring department they would work through the night making clothes for local funerals and there would be prayers every morning before work for the live-in staff.
Suits and costumes were made for ladies and gentlemen. I knew Mr. Jones who was head tailor there and every Saturday my mother would go there for her grocery and there was a Mr. Frank Phillips who specialised in different blends of tea and coffee. He started at the Emporium and then began his own business which was very successfully carried on by his son.
There was a dressmaking department run by a Mrs. Davies from way up the top of Llanbister and local girls used to serve their apprenticeships with her. You could get a blouse, skirt or dress made upstairs in her department. The drapery department was run by a Mrs. Cole and there was also a millinery department and I remember being taken there as a child by my father to buy a hat.
There was this big room with drawers all around it and inside each one were lovely hats for me to try on. In those days a hat cost about 10/- that's fifty pence in new money. I bought a lovely one once at Bon Marche in Middleton Street. It didn't cost much, only 2/11 in old money and for an extra 6d I had a little wreath of rosebuds to go on it as it was Easter time.
The Emporium was very famous at one time, people coming from all directions to shop there. We used to go to the bakery at A.G. Coates for our bread at Easter – hot cross buns which had a lot of fruit in them."

Miss M. Abberley

The Emporium Warehouse - Courtesy Of S. Collard

The following account is by Mrs. Caroline Walters (nee John) of Bedford who recalls life and work at the Emporium in 1914. Researched by Mrs. Ruth Jones.

Recollections of an Apprentice at the Central Wales Emporium - c. 1914.

"It gives me great pleasure in my 90th year to recall vividly and almost relive, my happy time at the Central Wales Emporium."

"This was a unique establishment with twelve departments and Mr. William Thomas was the sole proprietor. He was a gentlemen of high principles, and of an upright Christian character. He was also a great music lover, and was the choirmaster at the Presbyterian Church in Ithon Road. He would collect us apprentices in to his choir. We had invitations to entertain visitors from the larger hotels, and I remember singing "Men of Harlech" with great gusto, Mr. Thomas joining in the chorus with many gestures which made it very difficult to keep a straight face!"

"Wages were very low - if improving after two years one earned 2/6 a week (12.5p)! if you became a sleeve hand (able to make all fashions of sleeves) after 1 year you could earn 12/- (60p) per month. Of course we didn't pay for board and lodgings anywhere - we all "lived in". Boys and young men, and girls in separate quarters."

"We worked from 8.30 a.m. until 6 or 7 with 1.5 hours total for meals. The half day was Wednesday."

"We all had to take our turn to carry coal up from the cellar in a scuttle - (This gave us an opportunity to look around for any "perks" such as oranges, shoe polish and candles - these latter were very desirable)."

"Quite a few of the staff "lived in". In the dressmaking department there were seven girls under the supervision of Madame Moreton Davies who was very strict. For other departments, at least three of them including the Head of Department. Some of the departments, as far as I can remember, were Upholstery, Manchester (lines etc.), Haberdashery (hose, gloves threads etc.), Mantles, Millinery, Grocery. This last employed about seven men and errand boys."

"Mr. William Thomas was a vegetarian and a great walker. Every day he would take his daily walk around the lake. His apparel for this jaunt was a top coat known in the fashion world as an "Inverness", having a cape over the shoulders. He often wore galoshes, and was very careful of his health, and often gave advice to any of us who needed attention, e.g. a dose of quinine for colds! He often used to go out into the country to get orders. I remember one such journey (by car with a driver from Norton's garage) to Abbeycwmhir and then walking. It was a joke with us that he carried a pair of socks in his pocket and we were sure that he did not give them away. It was rumoured that he even carried a pair in his pocket on Sundays."

"We all had to take part in fire exercises. These took place from the "Governor's" bedroom. A long sack like a tube was fastened firmly to the floor by a strong chain. This was then thrown out of the bay window and secured at the other end. He would go first and then it was our turn. The bakery boys were there ready to catch each one. We all used to tie our skirts down with an elastic band to keep our frills from showing and too much leg! We would arrive on the pavement with great relief and many blushes. This exercise always took place in the early morning before breakfast, but even so quite often a crowd would gather to watch the fun.
Prayers were at 5 minutes to ten each evening. All the doors were locked and silence reigned. The Governor, as we were instructed to address him, would lead the prayers. We all knelt around a long dining table and sang a hymn. During the war one such hymn comes to mind - "For those in peril on the sea" and sometimes the Russian National Anthem - the first line being "God, the All Terrible". After prayers Mr. Thomas would walk to the door and with a smile, wish us all goodnight."

"It was his custom to make a nightly survey of the whole premises, from the cellar to the top warehouse, carrying a lantern that was already lit and handed to him by one of the kitchen staff."

"The 1914-18 War did not affect us young girls seriously, although the town was full of the RAMC regiment and many war casualties were arriving - some on stretchers. Many of these "took the waters" and were almost well again (this I have seen happen myself). After taking a dose of this "miracle water" and a run around the Spa grounds to work off the effects (there were "loos" in plenty spaced out in these grounds). A time came when conscription was in force. All the young lads that were called up were held in the Albert Hall overnight, ready to depart by train at 4.00 a.m. Even so, crowds turned up to wave farewell. Many of the smaller hotels were taken up for soldiers' billets and often invitations were issued to an evening at the piano or whist drives. A great enjoyment was to be taken by our boyfriends (mine was Harold Millward) up to the Cairn Tea Rooms, near the highest point of the Golf Links. Another treat was to hire a deck chair on the common overlooking the lake (no trees, then, to obscure the view)."

"After several years of serving my apprenticeship, I became appreciative of the way Mr. Thomas treated his staff. He was not a proud man, and no lover of luxury (for instance, his bedroom was very plain). It was a very happy establishment with plenty of good plain food, and supervised by an honourable gentlemen who was held in high esteem by all who knew him."

*I was told by an ex-employee that Mr. Thomas always liked to employ good looking staff and if they could also sing, they were almost sure to be engaged! - R.

The Emporium As It Stands Today - Copyright Joel Williams

THE NEW
Welsh Woollen Warehouse,
LLANDRINDOD WELLS,

For all makes of Genuine Welsh Goods at Wholesale Warehouse Prices.

A Grand Assortment of **Welsh Travelling Rugs**—genuine

Beautiful WELSH SHAWLS, manufactured on the Premises.

A large consignment of **Real Welsh Shawls**, variety of shades, at 6/11, worth 10/6, under cost of production, only to be had at this Warehouse.

Welsh Costume Tweeds, from 9¾d. Specially recommended.

Welsh Tweeds for Gents' Suits made up by experienced tailors on the Premises. Fit guaranteed.

Visitors are requested to call at the Warehouse before leaving the Town for Patterns of our Specialities.

—o—

W. THOMAS, *Manufacturer,*

Emporium Woollen Warehouse,

LLANDRINDOD WELLS.

Mr. J. O. Davies

"Mr J.O. Davies started his own business on the corner of Station Crescent and Middleton Street but before that he worked in Maple Stores grocery shop run by my relatives in Tremont Road. They also had a larger store with a bakery called Grosvenor Stores in the Ridgebourne."

Mr. Duff Edwards

Mr. J.O. Davies - Courtesy Of Mr. Idris Davies

J.O. DAVIES & SONS
FINE FOODS & WINES SPAR
MARLBOROUGH HOUSE, STATION CRESCENT
LLANDRINDOD WELLS, LD1 5BD
TELEPHONE: 01597 82 2114
OPENING HOURS 7 AM - 9 PM MON - SAT
FRESH SANDWICHES, FRUIT & VEG
FOR A SELECTION OF ORGANIC FOODS
GRAIG FARM

Grosvenor Stores

"My Grandfather built Grosvenor Stores and later my mother and father ran it and lived there when I was a child. Mr. J.O. Davies used to work there at one time, and ran the branch shop down Maple Terrace in Tremont Road. Of course he later went on to own his own shop in Middleton Street."

Mr. Duff Edwards

Motorbikes outside which is now Wallis, Courtesy Of Mr. Peter Knight

WALLIS OF LLANDRINDOD
LLANDRINDOD WELLS
TEL: 01597 82 2057
SUPPLIERS OF ELECTRICAL GOODS & MANY LABOUR SAVING APPLIANCES. STOCKISTS OF THE LATEST IN WIRELESS & TELEVISION APPARATUS.
RESIDENT IN TIMES BUILDINGS FOR 32 YEARS

Shops At Fiveways

"The area around Fiveways was quite busy. At Sunnycroft, which was a boarding house, there was a shop in the basement called Greenlands, stocking Furnishings, Millinery and ladies' wear. There was a tearooms at Fiveways, Bounds The Chemist and Frank Phillips a grocer who stocked beautiful coffee."

Miss M. Abberley

Spa Road & Temple Street

Copyright - Joel Williams

Temple Street

Copyright Joel Williams

'There were lots of cafes in town - Harpers, The Loui's Café, and Morgan Morris had three, one in Park Crescent, one in Station Crescent where the Bakehouse is now, and one in Temple Street. We used to be taken, as children, to parochial tea parties there. It was great fun with bun feasts for the boys! A lot of places around Llandrindod used to do meals and folk would walk out to places like Guidfa Farm, or the Cairn Tearooms on the Golf Links for a ham and egg supper."

Mr. Don Nelson

The Pop Factory

"There used to be a bottle pop factory at the back of what is now Somerfield, where they produced lemonade and ginger beer etc., in those old glass bottles with a marble in the top."

Mr. & Mrs. Duff Edwards

Miss Wilde

"Miss Wilde had a Tobacconist's shop in Temple Street, where the Radnor Travel Centre is now.
The shop was like a black hole with wooden floor boards and no electric light - I think she used to have a gas lamp."

(Note - this shop was open as late as the 1970's.)

Arcade Shops

"Where Ferndale Furnishers is today there was an arcade - before the cinema was there. It was a wonderful place for children with shops selling toys and games. You could also buy useful things like china, enamelware and household things. At Christmas it was magical and father used to take me on Christmas Eve to buy me something, not expensive things, but a game of snakes and ladders or a Snap or Happy Families card game."

Miss M. Abberley

Eadie's (Shoe Shop)

"Eadie's Shoe Shop was where I bought shoes and in those days they cost about £2-3".

Mr. Duff Edwards

"There were two shops in the Rock Park arcade - one an Irish linen shop which when it closed, was taken over by the British Legion. They closed too as the visitors got less and the waters had gone. At one time they'd sell 100 glasses of water by 7 o' clock in the morning."

"There also used to be two little shops in an arcade at the top of Rock Park - one was a linen shop run by a Miss MacCallum. She only opened in the summer months."

Mr. Saunders

Pump House At Rock Park

Copyright - Joel Williams

High Street

Copyright - Joel Williams

TRANSPORT

In times past, as readers will realise from the following memories, Llandrindod Wells was served extremely well by various forms of public transport.

Plas Winton Square

Copyright - Joel Williams

Middleton Street

Copyright - Joel Williams

Pony & Trap

"During the season there used to be little ponies and traps parked down on Gwalia Square and opposite the Commodore, as it is now. Some of the ponies pulled invalid carriages and they'd take visitors around the town and down to Rock Park."

Mr. D. Nelson

Penry Jones

"Mr. Penry Jones was a popular man in the town. He used to meet the trains with his horse and carriage and take visitors to their hotels and boarding houses. Later on he had cars for the job and his business premises were at the Vaga House in High Street."

Miss. M. Abberley

"We remember Mr. Penry Jones who used to run taxis and meet the trains at the station taking visitors to their hotels. The Pump House Hotel had its own service to transport its guests to and from the trains."

Mr. & Mrs. Duff Edwards

ITHON SADDLERY
MOBILE SHOP UNIT:-
OPERATING FROM,
"CAELY", PENYBONT,
LLANDRINDOD WELLS
POWYS, LD1 5SY
TELEPHONE/FAX:-
01597 82 4356

Mr. Penry Jones - Courtesy Of The Late Mrs. Adey

Transport

"When I worked at the Pump House Hotel in the 1920's we had horses and carriages fetching visitors from the station and taking them back again. There was a big carriage with two horses, a footman and a coachman and another horse and cart to carry luggage. We left the Pump House Hotel and came galloping down to the Automobile Palace - they couldn't do that today! - straight across and up Spa Road to the far side of the railway line for the London train at 10 o' clock in the morning."

"I worked there for ten years and I remember the Crosville Bus Company used to have buses here in Llandrindod. They ran services to Rhayader, Knighton and Builth several times a day but eventually these died out as more people got motorcars. Their depot was in Oxford Road behind the High Street fish & chip shop." (You can still see, very faintly, some writing on the brick wall of the Ystrad about carriages for hire.)

"I remember going down home to Hereford on a Crosville bus with solid tyres - and it was a rough ride as the roads had loose stones."

Mr. Jack Saunders

Crosville Buses Outside Emporium Square 1920's - Courtesy Of Ruth Jones

Memories of Transport

"There were three or four Charabancs around the town at one time taking visitors sightseeing. One was owned by Mr. Penry Jones, one by Arthur Adie, and another by Owens' in High Street."

"Mr. Tom Norton's bus, called "Colonel Bogey", took visitors to set points from Norton's corner at the Automobile Palace. They would go up to the Golf Links and the Cairn Tearooms. The visitors would walk around, enjoy the views, have tea and be brought back down to town again. They also used to run tours around the Elan Valley area."

"In the height of the season there were little ponies and traps parked down on Gwalia Square (outside the now Radnor District Council offices) which also took visitors about the area."

"There used to be an A.A. man called Ted McCoey who used to control traffic. He had a motorbike and sidecar and he would salute you as he went past, if you had a membership badge on your car. There was also an R.A.C. man in Llandrindod and he would salute you if you were an R.A.C member."

Mr. Jack Saunders

The A.A Man

"There used to be an A.A. man called Ted McCoey who directed traffic down at Fiveways by R.V.W. Edwards electric shop on the corner of Spa Road. He was called up during the war and no one replaced him."

Mrs. Kathleen Davies

The Railway Station 1900's - Courtesy Of Radnorshire Museum

Copyright - Joel Williams

Railway Journeys

"I remember you could travel to Shrewsbury from Llandrindod for 8 shilli[ngs] and 8 pence, which in today's money is about 45 pence. It was a favourite tri[p of] mine and I also used to go to Swansea on a straight through train. If you cau[ght] the 5.25 am mail train you could have a nice long day out and get back [to] Llandrindod at 6.00 p.m. I also remember the station Master who live[d at] Station House (next to the post office). During the summer because there w[ere] so many visitors coming by train they started collecting the tickets at Penybo[nt]

Wymans Book Stall

"There was a thriving book stall on the station and porters would hop off [the] train to buy newspapers for passengers. My father knew Mr. Ben Pugh who [ran] the stall so he bought his paper there too. He always took the Western M[ail]. There was a paper called "The Radnorshire Standard" - it was produce[d at] Caxton House in the High Street, where Sayce Printers are today."

Miss Mary Abberley

"There used to be trains to London which left Llandrindod at 10.00 in [the] morning and in the afternoon there was a 3 o' clock train which came fr[om] London bringing visitors from away to take the Spa Waters. Most of the ho[tels] had their own horse and carriage to pick up their guests and the footmen use[d to] wear three cornered hats and jackets with brass buttons. The pair of horses u[sed] to trot down the street with the carriage that took about six people. The visit[ors] came all through the season which ended in October."

Mr. Jack Saunders

Fish Train

"There were far more trains running when I was younger and at about 8.3[0 at] night the fish train came through from Swansea taking fish to Shrewsbury a[nd] the Midlands."

Mr. Duff Edwards

The Queen's visit in 1952

"...remember when her Majesty the Queen and the Duke of Edinburgh came to ...ndrindod in 1952. The visit was to officially open the Claerwen Dam in the ...n Valley near Rhayader. The evening before the visit the Daimler cars they ...re to use were on display at the Automobile Palace for all to see."

"...used to live at Kingswood in Tremont Road and the Royal Train was standing ...ow on the track, I could see the Queen's maids of honour arranging her ...thes hangers. Other people were preparing the carriages for her return from ... Elan Valley."

Miss Mary Abberley

"...hen the Queen visited Llandrindod our daughter was in a group of the Junior ...d Cross amongst other members of the public down by the station and my ...fe was standing opposite when she drove by in a Daimler car. The Queen was ...aring a lovely red outfit with black trimmings. I was on police patrol all day, ...ving up and down the road from the Elan Valley, Rhayader and Newbridge-...-Wye, making sure there was no trouble."

Mr. Duff Edwards

The Queen's Visit In 1952 - Courtesy Of Radnorshire Museum

The Queen's Visit In 1952 - Courtesy Of Radnorshire Museum

The Automobile Palace

The Automobile Palace, although retaining its original facade has been converted into separate business units - Greenstyle Cycles, Lakeside Design, The Sandwich Bar, Kensington Dress Agency and the local Job Centre.

The National Cycle Museum is also situated here and offers an interesting glimpse of the past to locals and visitors alike.

The Autopalace Copyright - Joel Williams

The Autopalace

"Mr. Tom Norton's business at the Automobile Palace was beautifully built with those lions along the top of the building. Several people worked there and they had a little bus called "The Colonel Bogey" to take visitors up to the Golf Links several times a day. It cost about 9 pence up and 6 pence down or something like that."

Miss M. Abberley

Courtesy Of The National Cycle Museum

The Golf Links

Day Trip To Aberystwyth

Mr. Saunders recalls an amusing and interesting tale of a bus trip taken in his younger days.

"In the early days they had what they'd call a charabanc. It had a canvas roof and a little door to go in and out. About three people could sit in a row and I remember going to Aberystwyth in it to play bowls."

"We got half way and I could feel it getting hot under my feet so I went and told the driver who stopped and checked, and would you believe it? The back axle was on fire! The driver was furious as someone was supposed to have checked it. There was a little pub near by and they gave us some water to put the fire out."

"We got to Aberystwyth in the end but he had no brakes at the back so it took a long time, anyway we got home alright but it was an uncomfortable ride with those old solid tyres."

Colonel Bogey

"They used to have a little bus called "Colonel Bogey" which used to go up to the Golf Links - 9d up and 6d back. It would take you up to the Cairn Café, right on top of the Golf Links. You could have tea there on a Sunday sitting outside to look at the view"

"It died down in the twenties as most people got cars. Until then only the doctors had cars and they were big, old fashioned two seater things."

Mr. Jack Saunders

Mr. Tom Norton - Courtesy Of The National Cycle Museum

During a recent conversation with Mr. Tom Norton junior, he told me a great deal concerning the family business, started at the turn of the 20th century by his father Tom Norton senior.

"Tom Norton who was born in Newtown on the 8th September 1870 worked for his half brother Clement for 1/- per week and in the late 1890's he decided to explore the "up and coming" Llandrindod Wells. He cycled frequently to the town on his "Grypto.""

"On the 1st March 1899 he opened his cycle & sports depot in the High Street. He was one of the first Raleigh dealers and he maintained a stock of some 200 bicycles. He offered to pay the train fare to any buyer travelling up to 100 miles."

"Cash takings on the opening day were £32, 3.6. Next day 2/-. During that year £2787/.16.0. The first petrol arrived in steel barrels and he acquired a Daimler Wagonette for 11 tourists followed by the first Commer Charabanc ever built."

"As the business expanded so rapidly in 1906 he decided that he needed a much larger property. In 1906 he purchased the land on which the Automobile Palace stands today at the high price of £1 per square yard, the vendor was Miss T Sheen. By 1911 the first (left hand) part was completed.

He then started trading under the name of Tom Norton Ltd. Which had an authorised capital of £15,000.
The remaining covered area (approximately 2/3rds) could not be completed until 1919 due to the First World War.
In 1925 the Automobile Palace Ltd. started trading. The face of the building was altered accordingly and Tom Norton Ltd. was wound up."

"Tom Norton envisaged an Aerodrome on the Rock Park Ddole during 1913. It never became one officially but the following are some of the events that took place:
Gustav Hamel - a wealthy Swede - landed on 6th October 1913.
The first air pageant promoted by Tom Norton took place in 1914 when Vivian Hewitt organised displays.
Many other events were organised after that, and in 1932 Sir Alan Cobham organised one of his well-known displays.
The museum at Llandrindod has much more information as, about 3 years ago, I donated a good deal of paperwork concerning local flying."

The Golf Bus - "Colonel Bogey"

"Tom Norton organised this in 1911. Its route to the Golf Club was via the Ridgebourne - the one official stop. The fare was 9d up and 6d down.
The first bus was a Model T Ford with an open body to seat about 11 persons. It ran on solid rubber tyres and had a chain driven rear axle. Some years later the vehicle was changed and a new (covered) body was fitted."

Colonel Bogey - Courtesy Of The National Cycle Museum

Courtesy of the National Cycle Museum

Great Western Cycle and Motor Depot,
LLANDRINDOD WELLS.

The largest and best equipped Sports Depot in the Principality.

Sole Maker of "Ariel" Golf Clubs and Balls.

Telegrams: "NORTON."

Telephone No. 17.

Bought of **TOM NORTON.**

Courtesy of the National Cycle Museum

The Flying Circus

"When I was a young trainee nurse at the hospital the flying circus came to t[he] Rock Ddole. I didn't tell mother but I had a ride on one of the planes a[nd] "looped the loop" over Newbridge. I was too scared to feel sick but it w[as] worth every penny, really wonderful!"

The Late Miss Annie Hutt

Air Shows At Rock Ddole

"When I was a boy the Alan Cobhams Air Show used to come to the Ro[ck] Ddole, taking people on trips over the town in old bi-planes. One of the[m] crashed into Rhyd Lyn Ddu Farm once, ran out of fuel and crashed right in[to] the front door of the guests' quarters, just below the "Welcome" sign. The[re] was a big photograph of it in the Daily Mirror."

Mr. Don Nelson

Courtesy of Radnorshire Museum

DAILY FLYING

At LLANDRINDOD WELLS

Commencing FRIDAY, AUGUST 3rd (until further notice)

SEASON 1933.

SEASON 1933.

THERE are now many provincial aerodromes in existence but not until this year has it been possible to establish regular flying in the heart of the Principality, although the Premier Welsh Spa has been gradually forging ahead in developing this exhilarating and modern form of travel.

Llandrindod Wells now possesses a centrally situated compact aerodrome (adjoining the Rock Hotel) of twenty-five acres and 550 yards long complete with hangarage to house a number of machines. Owners of private aeroplanes are therefore able to fly to Central Wales and even make it their base for daily tours over country so famous for its beauty. The landing fee is 2/0 per machine and the cost of hangar space per twenty-four hours 5/-. Fuel and oil supplies available on landing ground.

Commencing on Friday, August 3rd, Messrs. Universal Aircraft Services Limited will experiment with a daily flying service and are prepared to make short or extended air tours at reasonable charges in addition to providing joy rides over the immediate neighbourhood at very popular prices. For this purpose the following machines will be placed in commission :— (1) " Avro " 504K biplane seating pilot and two passengers ; (2) " Bristol " biplane fitted with 275h.p Rolls Royce Falcon engine, seating pilot and one passenger. **Rates:** in the " Avro " (two passengers) 9d. per mile each passenger or if one passenger 1/- per mile. In the " Bristol " (one passenger) 1/3 per mile. **JOY RIDES from 5/-**

The SCALE set out enables comparison to be made of flying and road mileages from which it will be observed that the cost is really no greater than car hire.

FARES.

To	Return Flying Mileage.	Return Road Mileage.	AVRO BIPLANE Two passengers (each) at 9d. Mile.	AVRO BIPLANE One passenger at 1/- Mile.	BRISTOL BIPLANE One Passenger at 1/3 Mile.
ABERYSTWYTH	68	95	£2 9 6	£3 6 0	£4 2 6
BIRMINGHAM	142	164	£5 6 6	£7 2 0	£8 17 6
BORTH	68	98	£2 11 0	£3 8 0	£4 5 0
BRISTOL	134	214	£5 0 6	£6 14 0	£8 7 6
CARDIFF	108	144	£4 1 0	£5 8 0	£6 15 0
CHESTER	140	170	£5 5 0	£7 0 0	£8 15 0
ELAN VALLEY LAKES (A spectacular flight of extreme interest.)	24	40	£— 18 0	£1 4 0	£1 10 0
HEREFORD	62	80	£2 6 6	£3 2 0	£3 17 6
LONDON	276	344	£10 7 0	£13 16 0	£17 5 0
SHREWSBURY	86	110	£3 4 6	£4 6 0	£5 7 6

For further information and booking of flights apply to Manager, The Aerodrome, Llandrindod Wells.

"Travel the Skyway for Business and Pleasure."

C. C. Hughes, Printer, Llandrindod Wells.

Pritchard's

"When I was young, as I remember the site was a big field where it was intended to build a Railway Hotel as the railway was flourishing then. Eventually, as nobody built a hotel Mr. Tom Pritchard bought the land to build a garage on. He asked my father if he knew anyone who would cut the long grass for him."

Miss M. Abberley

"I remember Pritchard's Garage. They were very good to me with repairs to my milk van. A gallon of fuel used to cost me eleven and a half pence in those days."

Mrs. Kathleen Davies

Pritchard's - Copyright - Joel Williams

ENTERTAINMENT & LEISURE

The Leisure activities and entertainment facilities of Llandrindod have, over the years, probably diminished due, in large, to the changing fortunes of Spa towns in general - so much of the past activities being solely part of the tourist package for the many visitors. Also the ever growing trend in TV and home entertainment of recent decades.

In the heyday of cinema, Llandrindod boasted three such establishments - Kino or Plaza (now Ferndale Furnishers in Middleton Street, the Pavilion and the Albert Hall. Today, we still have live entertainment at the Albert Hall with the local theatre group putting on pantomimes, dramas etc. The Pavilion also hosts live entertainment and of course we have the annual Victorian Festival which brings entertainers from other areas.

The sporting facilities are much as they were years ago - a thriving bowling scene and golf course still bring visitors to the town.

Various public houses offer entertainment from time to time as they did in the past, the Llanerch Inn being the oldest hostelry in Llandrindod, dating back to the sixteenth century.

The Pavilion
conference centre & theatre

The Pavilion

**The Pavilion
Llandrindod Wells
For
Excellent Conference
Facilities
and
a Superb Variety of Shows & Theatre**

For further details call

Tel: 01597 83532 Fax: 01597 824413
e-mail: pavilion@powys.gov.uk

The Grand Pavilion

"We used to go to the cinema at the Grand Pavilion. On a Wednesday and Saturday afternoons they had a matinee for the children, and then after six o' clock every night there would be a big film."

"I watched quite a few Charlie Chaplin films there but sometimes, just as you were getting really interested, the film would break and it usually took about half an hour to fix it. It was all silent films in those days and it only cost sixpence to sit downstairs or a shilling to sit in the balcony."

Mr. Jack Saunders

Grand Pavilion & Rock Park Hotel

"When I was working as a signwriter and poster designer, I used to do posters to advertise the dances and other events there, including the cinema. The police ball was held there every year, a very popular event, which cost half a crown to attend. If you didn't want to dance you could go up into the balcony and watch the dancers on the floor. Another annual dance was the Shilling Hop run by the conservatives. The Rock Park Hotel had marvellous dances on New Years Eve too!"

Mr. Duff Edwards

Work

"I was an apprentice signwriter when I left school with Ray Stimpson who had a studio in Princes Avenue. We used to do posters for the cinemas and Grand Pavilion events. When he finished I set up on my own but then I joined the Police Force and stayed in it until I retired in 1973. I was promoted in 1964 to Traffic Inspector in Newtown."

Mr. Duff Edwards

The Grand Pavilion

Copyright - Joel Williams

Cinemas

"Some of the best films I ever saw were at the Albert Hall - such as "Qu Vadis" and "The Fall of an Empress." The last film I remember there wa "Paris - The Next Best Thing." Of course in those days there were thre cinemas going - the Albert Hall, The Pavilion and The Kino, where Fernda Furnishers is now. There was a pianist down by one side of the screen anc remember seeing "Way Down East" there."

Mr. Duff Edwards

"In the 1940's they put plays on at the Kino. One theatre group was th McCoey girls. Mary McCoey was a local person but she used to act wi professionals like Dinah Sheridan, who later became quite famous."

Mrs. Edwards

The Kino

"Later when I was a child we had a cinematograph in Middleton Street calle the Kino. It was disinfected every day and the plush chairs were ve comfortable. I used to like "The Exploits of Elaine" as you had to guess wh would happen next week - if you got it right, you received a little prize."

Miss Mary Abberley

Grand Pavilion,
Llandrindod Wells.

Two Grand Miscellaneous

CONCERTS

on

Saturday, July 18th, 1931.

AT 3 P.M. and 8 P.M.

BY THE

PENTREPOTH SENIOR BOYS' SCHOOL CHOIR,

MORRISTON.

(Winners at the Llanelly National Eisteddfod, 1930 and Birmingham Musical Festival, 1931.)

Conductor - - Mr. IVOR E. SIMS.
Accompanist - - Mr. ELWYN A. REES.

Admission : 2/-, 1/- & 6d.
(Including Tax).

Sayce Brothers, Printers, Llandrindod Wells.

The Grand Pavilion Concert Poster - Courtesy of Powys Archives

LLANDRINDOD WELLS Thurs., April 22nd, for 3 days only
Matinee Saturday at 2-30

KNIGHTON, Monday and Wednesday, April 26 and 28.

PRESTEIGN, Tues., April 27.   Hay, Thurs., April 29—3 days

ELISABETH BERGNER

"AS YOU LIKE IT"

WITH   (U)

Laurence Olivier, Henry Ainley and Leon Quartermaine.
Directed by Dr. PAUL CZINNER.

The World's Greatest Actress in the World's Gayest Comedy

THE PRESS SAYS:

Miss Bergner has achieved the greatest performance in the film of the year—*Daily Mail*.

This is Bergner's Greatest Triumph—*Daily Mirror*

"As You Like It" sets a new standard for the screen—*Daily Telegraph*

ALSO IN THE SAME PROGRAMME

The "JONES FAMILY" in another of their truly amazing portrayels of the Happy (?) Family at home   **"EDUCATING FATHER"**
(U)

16

LANDRINDOD WELLS Monday, April 12th for 3 days only
KNIGHTON, Thursday and Saturday, April 15th and 17th
RHAYADER, Friday, April 16th.   HAY, Monday, April 19th

TOGETHER AGAIN !

WARNER BAXTER · MYRNA LOY
in
To Mary — with Love

IAN HUNTER
CLAIRE TREVOR
JEAN DIXON

From the story by Richard Sherman

20th CENTURY FOX

(A)

★ The SWEETHEARTS of "Strictly Confidential" and "Crooks in Clover" together again in a gallant and glorious film theme as real and sincere as anything you have yet seen ……… as different from the ordinary picture as night from day.

To you, with praise for a fine film, we commend "TO MARY WITH LOVE."

Also in the Same Programme

BRIAN DON LEVY and GLENDA FARRELL in

"HIGH TENSION" (U)

fast moving, crackling comedy with a laugh every minute ! THRILLS UNDERSEA ! High-Jinx Ashore ! ……… that's HIGH TENSION.

"SHOWBOAT" IS TERRIFIC

LLANDRINDOD WELLS Monday, Apr. 19th for 3 Days only
KNIGHTON, Thursday and Saturday. April 22th and 24th.
RHAYADER, Fri, Apr. 23rd.   HAY, Mon., Apr. 26th — 3 days

GEORGE ARLISS

kidnaps himself

tricks himself

and then triumphs

over himself

GEORGE ARLISS in
Great Dual Role

HIS LORDSHIP

A GAUMONT BRITISH PICTURE
Directed by
HERBERT MASON

ARLISS v. ARLISS . . .

The most astounding dual role ever played by any actor . . . .
The crowning achievement of a brilliant acting career . . . .
    SEE WHAT THE PRESS SAYS:
"There is enough unconscious humour in this film for a dozen full
        length comedies—" *The Times.*
"I consider it the finest Arliss has ever made."—*Daily Sketch.*
"You will love two ARLISSES for the price of one"
                                Sunday Dispatch.

SEE HANDBILLS for Special SUPPORTING PROGRAMME.

"SHOWBOAT" IS GIGANTIC.

THE PLAZA CINEMAS

(Where the Best Pictures Come and the Best People Go)

UNDER THE PERSONAL DIRECTION OF DESMOND J. MADIGAN

The Management reserve the right to alter this programme without notice.

LLANDRINDOD WELLS.

NIGHTLY CONTINUOUS from 6-45
(Unless otherwise stated).

MATINEE EVERY SATURDAY AT 2-30 P.M.

PRICES   1/6, 1/3, 1/- and 6d. (including tax).

Seats at 1/6 and 1/3 may be reserved without extra charge. Phone 167.
Reduced Prices for Children between the ages of 4 and 14.
CHILDREN IN ARMS will not be admitted.
Free Parking Ground for Patrons' Cars adjoining Cinema.

HAY.

NIGHTLY COMMENCING at 7.45 p.m.
SATURDAYS 8 p.m.

PRICES - 1/6, 1/3, 1/- and 6d. (including tax).

Seats at 1/6 and 1/3 may be reserved without extra charge. Phone 4.
Reduced Prices for Children under twelve.
Free Parking Ground for Patrons' Cars adjoining Cinema.

KNIGHTON.

Monday, Wednesday and Saturday at 7.45 p.m.
Thursday, 8 p.m. Matinee on Saturday when specially noted.

Admission: 1/3, 1/- and 9d. Children: 9d. and 6d.
(including tax).

RHAYADER.

Every Friday,
Commencing at 8 p.m.
Unless otherwise stated.
PRICES AS KNIGHTON

PRESTEIGN.

Every Tuesday commencing
at 8 p.m.
Unless otherwise stated.
PRICES AS KNIGHTON.

C. C. Hughes, Printer, Llandrindod Wells.

The Lake

The lake was created from a stretch of marsh land by damming the outflow stream. The present day boathouse was built in the 1990's on the same site as the 1908 building. The lake has been used for over a hundred years for recreational purposes such as boating and fishing. It offers interest to naturalists and ornithologists alike, especially during the spring when thousands of toads arrive from surrounding areas to breed. The local Radnorshire Wildlife Trust has been recording their activities for many years.

"A lot of boating used to take place on the lake until the fishing seemed to take over. Some boats were big enough to take quite a few people, others were small rowing boats and canoes which myself and my mother could row."

"There was no café there in the early days - just a boathouse and I remember my father being terribly upset when one of the managers fell and was killed whilst putting up a flagpole for some special celebration or Coronation."

"I remember the Regattas, which seemed to die out over time. That was quite a day's enjoyment as there was a prize, a leg of mutton I think. The first person to swim out to the island won it."

Miss M Abberley

New Tea Rooms Being Built - Copyright Joel Williams

The Old Tea Rooms

The New Lakeside Cafe - Copyright Joel Williams

The Lake And Pump House Hotel

Rock Park Spa

The Rock Park Spa set in 18 acres of wooded parkland offered the visitors of a century ago a wide range of summer entertainment - and of course the Spa waters.

Today, the refurbished Spa centre can offer the services of many and varied alternative therapies plus the waters and a restaurant.

Spa Waters

"The Chalybeate waters were free, but down at the Pump House in Rock Park you had to pay. They would also deliver it in big stone jars to the visitors' hotels or apartments. There were several doctors residing in town who just advised people on what course of water to take."

Miss M Abberley

Rock Park Spa Pavilion

Copyright - Joel Williams

The Llanerch Inn - Courtesy Of Radnorshire Museum

Copyright - Joel Williams

The Llanerch Inn

"The Llanerch is one of the oldest buildings in Llandrindod. It used to be run by the Lewis family who had several sons and daughters, all employed on helping to carry out the duties of running a public house. I used to go down there sometimes for a meal which cost half a crown - which is equivalent of twelve and a half pence today."

"In May, a fair was held on the Llanerch field where Setten & Durward's factory is today. I'd sometimes go in the evening and during the day the children loved the slides and hoopla."

Miss M Abberley

Setten & Durwards - Copyright Joel Williams

"The Llanerch used to keep their own pigs for ham and bacon to use in the meals for the visitors.
They employed a man to go around the hotels to collect waste food for the pigs. It was boiled up and made into pig swill."

Kathleen Davies

"The Llanerch was run by the Lewis family. The beer was good and only cost fourpence half penny and cider was threepence half penny, and my five woodbine cigarettes were only a penny."

Mr. Jack Saunders

The Llanerch
16th Century Inn

Llandrindod Wells

- Ideal touring base for Mid-Wales
- Character bar with three traditional ales
- Outside patio and beer garden with children's play area
- Excellent selection of meals at lunchtime and during the evening
- Dining room for special occasions, functions and Sunday lunches
- 12 bedrooms, with en-suite facilities, colour TV, all have coffee/tea-making equipment, radio and telephone

A welcome for all the family

Ring now on 01597 822086

CAMRA and Good Pub Guides

The Middleton Arms

"The Middleton Arms was run by a Mrs. Powell who had one daughter called Kitty. She had a lovely dolls house and lots of dolls kept in a little shed at the back and I used to go round there to play. Mrs. Powell ran a very tidy public house and there was never any trouble there. Next door was a blacksmiths shop, Charles Jones, he kept a horse and carriage for hire."

Miss Mary Abberley

The Middleton Arms - Courtesy of Radnorshire Museum

The Middleton Arms as it stands today
Copyright Joel Williams

Carnival

"The annual carnival was a big event and when I was a boy they used to close Middleton Street for the confetti battle on the night of the carnival. There would be a few stalls selling confetti and we'd throw it at everybody and put it down girl's necks."

"They were first rate carnivals in those days and my family usually entered in some way or another. I remember in the 1930's I entered as a Gondolier with my father's old Standard car, a 1924 model which he'd bought from Norton's Garage. It was off the road and unlicensed so I had to get permission from the police to enter it. I dressed it up as a gondola using timber battening, crepe paper and anything I could lay my hands on. I festooned it with lots of rambling roses and won a prize with it."

Mr. Duff Edwards

Broadway

"I lived in Nelson Street for some time and the football ground was at the back, they called it Dinam grounds, where Maxwell Engineering and the Carpet Factory are now. I could see half of the ground from upstairs so I used to watch half a football match!"

"It was awfully wet there so they moved it later up to Lant Avenue. Where the football & rugby club is now. It used to be an old rubbish tip which they filled in with soil."

"I can remember when there was only half a dozen houses up Broadway. The Broadway House Hotel was there but it was a long way up before you came to another house."

Mr. Saunders

Football

"There were two football teams in Llandrindod - the Crossing team and the Llandrindod team. The Dinam was the football field, below Waterloo Road and it was screened off from the road by big corrugated sheets to stop you watching from there."

"I recall one match, against Merthyr Tydfil I think, when the shout went up that a boy was drowning in the brickyard pool - well everyone - two hundred people at least all rushed to help with the rescue then returned to play the match."

Mr. D Nelson

Llandrindod AFC 1927-28

This is the team which played Aberdare 6th Welsh Cup - losing 4-2 at Aberdare

They reached SF Welsh Amateur cup losing to top amateur team Lovel ATM 3-1 the same season where there were 1,200 people at the Dinam.

Back Row - ? Harold Edwards, Len Chrimes, M Mills, W H Mills, Mr Giles (Frontiers)

Middle Row - Penry Jones, Ernie Porter, Jim Meveich, B Evans, Ginger Matthews, Ned Charles - John's father, Tom Jones

Front Row - Tommy Davies (saddler), Hector James, Tom Davies, Rod Jones, Tommy Dee, Billy Bird.

We end our trip down memory lane back in the area of the Crossing, with recollections of the old Baptist Chapel in Waterloo Road, and the shops in Tremont Road.

"The old Baptist Chapel in Waterloo Road was bought by Mr. Griff Evans - eventually he knocked it down and rebuilt it into a bungalow. There is still a stone plaque in the front saying that the Foundation stone of the Chapel was laid by the Squire of Penybont Hall, Percy Severn."

Miss M Abberley

"Mr. Griff Evans bought the chapel and rebuilt it into a bungalow - he had enough bricks left over to build another house in Tremont Road as you go out towards Crossgates. When it was a chapel, the caretaker used to live in the basement."

Mr. Saunders

Copyright - Joel Williams

"Our house, (Beech Grove), had a dairy at the back of it when Tommy Hope lived here. After milking the cows, the milk would be cooled and sold - Tommy Hope also had a haulage contractors business."

"We also remember shops down the crossing and elsewhere. Dedmans had a fish and chip shop in what is now part of Hodges' shop, Joe Hodges had a grocer's shop, which, at the time, was next door. Harold Millward also had a grocer's shop where the crossing now has a hairdressers. Jack Mostyn had a butcher's shop next door, which is now a private house, Bessie Abberley had a grocers shop and post office where we now have the Crossing Fish and Chip shop, and also, Edwards had yet another grocer's shop down Maple Terrace."

"They used to bring freshly baked bread down to this shop which was baked at their other shop up the Ridgebourne, which is now Grosvenor Stores. "Deans" the sweet shop in the Ridgebourne was a real treat. Mrs. Dean used to weigh sweets out of several jars for us to have a mixture for a few pennies."

"We also remember Moss's shop, another grocer's, and Moorehouse's, the butchers up the Ridgebourne. Part of the Railway building was another shop, which was open-fronted - and called Wyman's the paper shop."

Mr. & Mrs. Bumford

Copyright - Joel Williams

The End.

Joel Williams

HUGE SELECTION OF QUALITY GREETINGS CARDS

SPLENDID SELECTION OF SWISS & BELGIAN CHOCOLATES

HEAPS OF PARTY THINGS AND HELIUM BALLOONS
AT THE

Candyman

SPA ROAD,
LLANDRINDOD WELLS

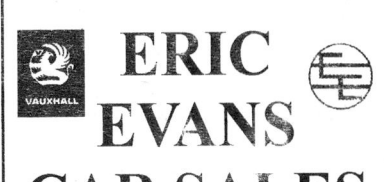

ERIC EVANS CAR SALES

VAUXHALL

VAUXHALL CAR &
VAN SALES SERVICE,
PARTS &
ACCESSORIES
CAR HIRE

STATION CRESCENT,
LLANDRINDOD WELLS
POWYS LD1 5BE
(01597) 82 4797

Changes - Nearly New

or give us a call on 01597 82 5283
For all your family needs. come on in and look at our everchanging range of locally crafted
Fleece blankets and hats.
Special offers on Nappies & Baby Wipes and a Nappy Changing area provided.
Concessionary coffee available while you browse,
and a play area for Children
OPENING HOURS
Mon, Tues & Thurs 9.30 - 3pm
Fri 9.30 - 4.00 pm
Sat 10.00 - 1.00 pm

PORTICUS
Fine Arts and Crafts
Rosemary Studman

No 1 Middleton Street, Llandrindod Wells, Powys
Telephone: 01597 823989

CRAFTS COUNCIL SELECTED

SPECIALISING IN WORK BY WELL-KNOWN DESIGNER WORKERS

```
        Jarol
      Kingcole
       Sirdar
        Tivoli
       Wendy
```

Bon Marche

(Prop. Mrs M Price)
Middleton Street
LLandrindod Wells
Powys LD1 5ET
Tel: 01597 822328

**Fabric, Craft, Haberdashery,
Dry Cleaning Agent**

LEWIS'S SHOE STORE

PORTLAND HOUSE,
LLANDRINDOD WELLS
TELEPHONE : 01597 82 2358
OPPOSITE HOTEL COMMODORE

CALL IN
AND SEE
OUR
EXTENSIVE
RANGE OF
FOOTWEAR
AND BAGS

ALL AT LOW
AFFORDABLE
PRICES

VERZON BOOKS & GALLERY

MIDDLETON STREET,
LLANDRINDOD WELLS
TEL:01597 82 5171

WISHES JOEL WILLIAMS
EVERY SUCCESS WITH THIS
BOOK. WE CAN COMPLETE
A COMPUTERISED
SEARCH TO HELP YOU
FIND OUT MORE
INFORMATION ABOUT
THE BOOK/S YOU REQUIRE

QUALITY FURNITURE AT COMPETITIVE
DISCOUNT PRICES

A COMPLETE RANGE OF HOUSEHOLD
FURNITURE TO SUIT ALL BUDGETS
* MODERN & REPRODUCTION FURNITURE
* 3 PIECE SUITES
* BEDS & BEDROOM FURNITURE
* OCCASIONAL PRICES
  FREE LOCAL
  DELIVERY
  OPENING HOURS
  MON-SAT
  9-5.30

Ferndale Furnishers
LLANDRINDOD WELLS
(01597) 823550
MIDDLETON STREET, LLANDRINDOD WELLS, POWYS LD1 5DG

If you want to stay put, contact........

Arvon House,
Temple Street
Llandrindod Wells
Powys
LD1 5DP
Tel: (01597) 824040
Fax: (01597) 823552

Radnor Care & Repair is an advisory service supporting older or disabled people living in their own homes. Advice is available on adaptations, improvements, repairs and welfare rights. Why not call in to see us?

...............But if you need a new home, contact.......

Mid Wales Housing Association is a Registered Social Landlord with properties throughout Powys, including Llandrindod Wells. Give us a call to find out more.

Mid-Wales Housing Association Ltd
Bryn Aderyn The Bank
Newtown, Powys SY16 2AB
Tel: 01686 627476
Fax: 01686 623195
Maintenance Direct Line: 01686 621662

Chris's Ladies' Fashionwear

- *Lingerie / Accessories*
- *Hats for Sale and Hire*
- *Stylish Daywear / Wedding / Parties or just for that Special occasion*

Temple Street, Llandrindod Wells,
Tel: 01597 822649
Alteration service available

Morgan & Co.

INDEPENDENT ESTATE AGENTS, VALUERS, AUCTIONEERS, SPECIALISING IN THE SALE OF TOWN & COUNTRY PROPERTIES THROUGHOUT POWYS AT REALISTIC PRICES, WITH COMPETITIVE FEES.
WINCHESTER HOUSE,
TEMPLE STREET
LLANDRINDOD WELLS
POWYS
LD1 5DL
TEL: 01597 82 5682

GRIFFIN LODGE HOTEL

DAINTRY INVITES YOU TO STAY IN HER SMALL LICENCED VICTORIAN HOTEL. COMFORTABLE BEDROOMS, MOST WITH EN-SUITE FACILITIES ETC. ENJOY OUR FRIENDLY WELCOME & GOOD HOME COOKING.
TEMPLE STREET,
LLANDRINDOD WELLS
TEL: 01597 822432

L & J WATSON

No.1 PARK CRESCENT
LLANDRINDOD WELLS
TELEPHONE:
01597 82 2087

BRITISH MEAT

HAIR TECHNIQUE UNISEX SALON

MIDDLETON STREET
LLANDRINDOD WELLS
TELEPHONE: 01597 82 2668

RIDGEBOURNE STORES
& POST OFFICE
M.W. & S.M. YEO
GROSVENOR ROAD,
LLANDRINDOD WELLS
POWYS LD1 5NA
TEL: 01597 82 2626

NEWSAGENTS,
TOBACCONISTS,
& GENERAL STORES
TOYS & FISHING TACKLE

S.G. MARSHALL
B.Sc. (HONS) (M.B.C.)

**OPTHALMIC OPTICIAN
CONTACT LENS
PRACTITIONER
PERSONAL EYE
CARE FOR
ALL THE FAMILY
MIDDLETON STREET,
LLANDRINDOD WELLS
TELEPHONE:
01597 82 3400**

J. & E.J. LEWIS

**GROSVENOR STORES,
WELLINGTON ROAD,
LLANDRINDOD WELLS,
TEL NO 01597 824369**

**BUTCHERS, BAKERS
& GROCERS
WHOLESALE, CATERING
& RETAIL
CAKES & BREAD
BAKED DAILY
ALSO ORGANIC BREAD
A SPECIALITY**

BUILDER CENTRE
HALL & CO

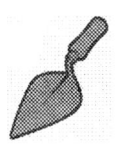

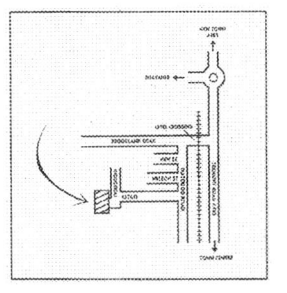

**HOW TO FIND US!
BUILDERS CENTRE (HALL & CO)
WATERLOO ROAD INDUSTRIAL ESTATE
LLANDRINDOD WELLS, POWYS LD1 6BH
TELEPHONE: 01597 82 4567
FAX: 01597 82 4605
OPENING TIMES: MON - FRI 7.30AM - 5.00PM
SAT 8.00AM - 1.00PM**

WILMANS PET CARE
(INCORPORATING RIDGEBOURNE)
PET SUPPLIES
WELLINGTON ROAD,
LLANDRINDOD WELLS
01597 82 4028

UNDER NEW MANAGEMENT
WIDE RANGE OF FOOD
TREATS, TOYS & EQUIPMENT
FOR ALL YOUR PET NEEDS.
WE ARE OPEN:
MON-SAT 9.00AM - 5.30PM
HALF DAY CLOSING ON
WEDNESDAY.
LATE NIGHT SHOPPING
ON FRIDAYS UNTIL 6.30PM
"YOUR PET IS OUR CONCERN"

BRADLEY'S MICA HARDWARE
E.M. BRADLEY & SON

LLANFAIR HOUSE, MIDDLETON STREET,
LLANDRINDOD WELLS, POWYS, LD1 5ET
0159782 2310

PAINTS & DECORATING
SUNDRIES

A. & M. MILLWARD
TUDOR LANE HOUSE,
2 MIDDLETON STREET, LLANDRINDOD WELLS
TELEPHONE / FAX: 01597 82 2048

FLOOR COVERINGS & SOFT FURNISHING
SPECIALISTS CURTAINS, BLINDS,
FABRICS AND ACCESSORIES

TV   Satellite

HITACHI

ROY MORGAN

LLANDRINDOD WELLS,
POWYS

TELEPHONE
01597 822258

AIWA   retra

KIDS KLOBBA
CORNUCOPIA
3 CRAIG ROAD
LLANDRINDOD WELLS
01597 825855

FROM TOTS TO TEENS

ACCESSORIES
& SCHOOL WEAR

PARTY PLAN AVAILABLE
PRAM & COT HIRE

OAKLEY'S CATERING SUPPLIES
WATERLOO ROAD, LLANDRINDOD WELLS

WE SUPPLY - AMBIENT / DRY, CHILLED,
FROZEN AND NON-FOOD PRODUCTS
CRISPS, SOFT DRINKS
AND CONFECTIONERY

FREE DELIVERY OR CASH & CARRY
PLEASE CALL ON: 01597 82 2366

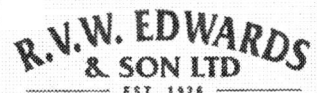

R.V.W. EDWARDS & SON LTD
EST. 1926

Radio, Television, Electrical
Retailers and Engineers

ASTRA SATELLITE TELEVISION

We provide a complete Television and Electrical Service

SATELLITE T.V. INSTALLATIONS & T.V. AERIALS

RETUNING & RECONNECTING VIDEOS & T.V.'S TO OUR LOCAL SIGNALS

SERVICING OF TELEVISIONS & VIDEOS

RECONNECTING COOKERS • LIGHT FITTINGS
WALL BRACKETS • BATHROOM HEATERS

WIRING ADDITIONAL LIGHTS & POWER POINTS

Fiveways
Llandrindod Wells
Telephone:
(01597) 822139

TEMPLE TILES

KEN & CECILY
HOLE (ARE RETIRING)
AND WOULD LIKE
TO THANK
CUSTOMERS
& FRIENDS
FOR THEIR SUPPORT
OVER 20 YEARS
BEST WISHES TO ALL

SANDWICH BAR
01597 82 4269

OPENING TIMES:
8.00 TILL 4.00
MONDAY - SATURDAY
WIDE SELECTION OF
ROLLS & BAGUETTES
BUSINESS LUNCHES
SUPPLIED

THE FISH BAR

HIGH STREET,
LLANDRINDOD WELLS.
TEL NO: 01597 822589
TRADITIONAL FISH & CHIPS,
PIES, PASTIES, SAUSAGES,
ALL BURGERS, CHICKEN,
FRESHLY COOKED CHICKEN
& DONNER KEBAB,
PLUS VEGETARIAN SELECTION
POP, SWEETS
AND MUCH, MUCH MORE
OPENING HOURS:

TUE - FRI:	11.30 - 14.00
	16.45 - 22.00
SAT:	11.30 - 14.00
	16.45 - 21.00

DILWYNS SOLICITORS

Temple Chambers,
Llandrindod Wells,
Powys
LD1 5DH
Tel: (01597) 822707
(4 lines)
Telefax: (01597) 824085

A comprehensive and efficient legal service
from one of the leading law firms in Mid Wales.
* Residential & commercial conveyancing
* Wills, estate & inheritnce tax planning
* Matrimonial & family matters
* Company law * Agricultural law
* Accident & other Civil litigation
Copyright/ patents law
* Debt recovery

28,000 *financial* products.

4,000 *mortgages*.

164 *unit trust* companies.

Or 1 phone call

We also provide no-nonsense unbiased
advice and personal service on all your
essential lifelong financial needs. With
no obligation to buy. Simply contact

HAYDN LEWIS FINANCIAL SERVICES
2A TEMPLE STREET,
LLANDRINDOD WELLS,
POWYS LD1 5DL
TEL: 01597 824338 (office)
Fax: 01597 825787

DBS FOR INDEPENDENT FINANCIAL ADVICE

A Member of DBS Financial Management PLC which is regulated by the Personal Investment Authority
FROM THE UK'S LARGEST PROVIDER OF INDEPENDENT FINANCIAL ADVICE